Swing Trading

Strategies

Master the Art of Swing Trading: Proven Techniques for
Profiting in Volatile Markets

William J. Stone

Table of Contents

How Swing Trading Works

T he financial market, forex trading is on the spot can make riches. All you need are the skills, a better understanding of the trade of your choice, the money to invest, and the personality that will fit in with your trade. Those are just a few of the requirements. Swing trade is a trade that can make you riches in a matter of a short period, and also you can lose a lot via the same route. This, however, should not be a scare. Of the years, I have known the forex market; swing trade can be ranked high. It is moreover the commonest mode of trade of the forex trades. Swing trade is the trading strategy that involves purchasing stocks at a lower price and selling them off at a higher price over a short period of time. This chapter will focus on what is swing trading and how it works for your better understanding. Swing trade falls in the category that's right between day trading and trend trading. This definition, however, is based on time. Day trading may take from few seconds to a day but not anything more than a day. Trend trading will take weeks to months. Swing trade will fall between since it's the trade of positions from seconds to about a few weeks but not for more than that. Swing trade uses the fluctuations in the trends and makes small profits from these changes, and by doing so, it clears losses quickly. The profits might seem small, but accumulatively over time, they are quite a sum. A swing is a move; it involves capturing these moves by enduring small pain as you wait for gains and then exit before pressure builds up and carries away all the small gains you had collected.

Swing traders deal with tradable assets — stocks; however, a problem sets in on when to get hold of the asset — buy; and when to let it go — sell; after it has gained them some profit. To get information about the asset or position, these traders use technical analysis. Technical analysis involves forecasting to which direction prices follow via the critical study of the past data of the market, the price history, and volume. With these data, the swing traders can now make a move on the trade. With swing trade, perfect timing is nothing to worry about; you only focus on the small gains, which will accumulatively make something big. Market charts have the support and resistance that define the trade, swing trade. Swing trade revolves between support, the area on the chart that has the potential buying pressure, and resistance; the opposite of support, which is the area on the chart that shows potential selling pressure.

How It Works

Firstly, you put the finger on a range market, one that is promising. To identify this, technical indicators are of importance, and that's where you focus. Use support and resistance levels; they play an important role since they will give a signal on whether to purchase the stock or not. That's not all, the bullish and bearish patterns show price points, and through their analysis, they can tell you where you should enter the stocks and where to exit from the stocks; they give signals on the entry points and exit points. Once the market is clear, then make sure to spot the right stocks. I would tell you; the best choices are the large-cap stocks; they swing high and low; they experience both extremes.

Technical indicators include:

- MAs (moving averages), they refer to lines that are after calculations of past prices. They help identify trend strength in that the farther away from the current price of a stock and trend falls, the weaker the trend. It helps you pinpoint spots for entry and exits.

- Relative strength index (RSI), this indicator provides a relative evaluation of how strong a price is by analyzing the past performance and the volatility. The scale runs from 1-100. It is best to check on the few sub-indicators here.

- Volume, it's an indicator that overlooks leading and lagging trends. It tallies trades, also gauges bulls and bears, and ensures they are both in control.

- Momentum indicators, on the other hand, are responsible for analyzing and evaluating the speed of price over a period of time, the rate of change.

- Mean reversion indicators will measure the length or distance a price will swing before it comes into contact with a counter impulse, which triggers a retracement, a temporal reversal of a comprehensive trend in the price of a stock.

- Trend indicators will overlook the direction which the market is taking, is it moving up, down, sideways, etc. It is a timely analysis, however.

Once you internalize the indicators and use them precisely and accurately, they go a long way and will help you in swing trading. These indicators will help you understand the market and plan for it. Swing traders will spend evenings analyzing the charts and trends as they look for these indicators so as to determine the fate of their investments on the trade or security. These indicators, however, require time to understand them. Use tutorials and applications to understand them and know how to spot them and use them.

Secondly, buy the stock and wait. Wait patiently as you monitor the charts. Here the price is waited to break just below the support. What makes best swing traders are the instincts and firm decisions without any regret. Once you get in, it means you are ready for anything, and so all you can do is monitor the curves as you wait for that moment that the price will break just below the support. When it does, hold on for a strong rejection of the price and then go to the next open candle. Move from candle to candle, monitoring the charts.

Thirdly is planning the exit strategy. You then set up your stop loss and take off with your profits before you reach the resistance. This is done just at the candle low. ATR is, however, a technical analysis form of an indicator that is responsible for measuring the volatility of the market on target. It decomposes a whole range of security or asset price for a certain period. With the help of ATR, you can visualize your exit.

A successful swing trader would advise you to find stocks that will be worth the while. Commonly these stocks are found in the upcoming catalysts. Upcoming catalysts that would look good include scheduled events like earnings reports, economic data points, among others. They pose the advantage that they are known ahead of time, and another juicy characteristic is that they happen regularly and timely; weekly, monthly, quarterly, etc. As a swing trader that is alert, its best to keep track of such money-blowing events, and you will make fortunes out of them. An analysis of such events will keep you ahead of time, and when the entrance point reveals itself, you just dive in and the out when you find the perfect time to leave.

The advantages and benefits of swing trading include the following. Firstly, it requires less time to monitor your trades in a day as opposed to day trading that requires a daily approach and analysis. Here you only need a few minutes, and you will manage your trades nicely and effectively on a daily basis, therefore, providing time to engage in other events in the day. Secondly, swing trade is able to maximize those short-term profit potentials; it achieves this by getting hold of the bulk that exists of the market swings. It, therefore, makes this trade profitable within a short time. Thirdly, swing traders can focus only on the technical analysis for information on trends, unlike day trading or some other trades that require both technical and fundamental analysis. This simplifies the process of trade. Lastly, another advantage is that swing trading exposes plenty of time, which can be used to place trades and even better, larger targets that will make the trade worthwhile eventually. The cons of swing trading include the following. Firstly, trade positions are prone and subject to risks that take place during weekends or even overnight. It is, however, a blow if they are unpredictable. Secondly, sudden changes in the market, especially market reversals, can result in huge losses. Abrupt market changes are invisible but expected once in a while. When they strike, substantial losses are felt all over. Thirdly, swing traders may end up losing long term trends that would make a great fortune, but due to early exits, they end up losing the trends. They favor short time deals and therefore lose more on the long-term trends. However, it is not always that a long-term trend will give great fortune; it might also fail you and give you a huge blow.

Tools and Platforms for Swing Trading

T rading platforms provide traders with the opportunity to place trades and monitor their accounts. There is a variety of platforms available to swing traders. They come with a number of different features. These include premium research functions, a news feed, charting tools, and even real-time price quotes. These additional features and tools enhance a trader's performance and make it easier to execute trades faster and accurately. Most platforms available today are designed for different financial instruments like Forex, stocks, futures, and options.

We basically have two different types of platforms. These are commercial platforms and prop platforms. Commercial platforms are mostly used by traders such as swing traders, retail investors, and day traders. They are largely easy to use and come with a myriad of features such as charts and a news feed.

We also have prop platforms. These are platforms that are customized for specific users, such as institutional investors and large brokerage firms. Apparently, their needs are much different compared to those of small traders and retail investors. The prop platforms are designed to take into consideration the different needs of these special clients.

As a swing trader, you will most likely use commercial platforms provided by different brokerage firms. Even then, there are some things that you need to be on the lookout before choosing one.

When selecting a platform, always watch out for the fees charged. As a small-scale retail swing trader, you want to trade on one that charges low and affordable fees. However, sometimes there are certain trade-offs. For instance, some platforms charge low fees, but they lack certain crucial features or provide poor services. Others may seem expensive but provide crucial features, including research tools and excellent services. Hence, you will need to consider all these factors before eventually selecting a suitable trading platform.

There is yet another crucial point to keep in mind when selecting a trading platform. Some platforms are available only through specific brokers or intermediaries. Other platforms are universal and work with different brokerage platforms and intermediaries across the board. Traders also select trading platforms based on their own personal styles and preferences. Some platforms are designed for specific financial products like options trading, day trading, currency trading, swing trading, and so on. As a trader, you should find out if a platform is compatible with your trading style. Therefore, do have the product in mind at all times. Geography is also a consideration in some cases because some platforms are only available to traders in certain jurisdictions and not others.

Type of Accounts

You will also need to complete additional paperwork that will allow you to short securities.

You will need to decide which type of account makes the most sense for you and your personal financial situation and whether you want to go short as well as go long. These are things you can always change or add later, so if you are not sure, start with the basics.

Commissions and Fees

Comparing broker commissions can be a little confusing. Many offer a flat fee that will typically range between $5.00 to as high as $25.00 per trade.

Other brokers will charge a fee based on how many shares you purchase or sell (with a minimum charge). An example of this type of fee would be $0.005 per share with a $1.00 minimum. Therefore, if you purchased 1,000 shares of a stock, it would cost you $5.00 in commission.

Platforms and Tools

Some of the more powerful broker platforms will also have tools that do technical analysis and studies that will find the price and volume patterns. These tools will identify and flag them for your consideration. While these can be helpful in making a trading decision.

If you do not have an account, I recommend that you do some research on a site like StockBrokers.com and find a platform that offers the following:

Research: some platforms will provide exclusive research reports to subscribers. Much of the research you need is available online, so I do not put much value on this factor.

Education: there are brokers that will offer some tutorials on how to use their platform and maybe even some basics regarding stocks and trading. These are nice to have but are not critical since the platform should be designed for ease of use and there are many resources available to better understand swing trading (such as this book you are reading!)

Mobile access: having mobile access is "nice to have" but, as a swing trader, generally speaking, you should not be making trades on the fly. With that said, mobile access to your trading platform can be an asset on occasion.

Scanning tools: you will also need a way to scan for buying opportunities. Fortunately, you do not necessarily need a real-time scanner like Trade Ideas, which is a tool that a day trader would utilize.

Alerts: the brokerage should provide an alert service that sends a text or email to a client when a certain event occurs. For example, if you are watching a stock for a good entry price, you can set an alert and then quickly act if needed, without letting an opportunity pass you by.

Tools Available Online

Finviz (finviz.com): The website name is short for Financial Visualizations. This site provides a massive amount of information on the stock market, different sectors, currencies, etc. It further provides financial analysis, research and data visualization, as well as excellent scanning tools.

ChartMill (chartmill.com): This site offers much of the same information provided by Finviz. The site also has a proprietary rating feature that gives a grade on a stock's situation and rates the quality of the setup if a trader is considering entering a position. This is another excellent site to find investment opportunities.

StockCharts.com (stockcharts.com): This is another excellent website that contains information similar to that offered by Finviz including charting tools, research data, commentary, and education.

Estimize (estimize.com): The site has an excellent calendar which can be used to see the upcoming company, government, and industry announcements that might move individual stocks, market sectors or the market overall.

StockTwits (stocktwits.com): Anyone can join and share their thoughts and ideas related to different securities. There are many worthless posts, but the site does offer a way to see what is trending and actively trading.

CNBC (CNBC.com): CNBC is a provider of business news and real-time market coverage.

Yahoo Finance (finance.yahoo.com): A quick go-to website for business news, commentary, and real-time quotes.

The websites listed above are only a few of the sites that a swing trader can utilize to find trading opportunities.

The services and information presented here were available as of the writing. Be aware that the owners of these websites may change the service levels and information they provide at any time.

Trading platforms are the actual platforms or software programs that enable traders to place their trades and monitor their accounts. An electronic trading platform is a computer program or a website with a user interface where traders place financial trades.

As a swing trader, you will use this platform to enter, close, exit, and manage your positions. This is often done via an intermediary such as your broker. Most traders use online platforms which are overseen and offered by brokerage firms. Brokers charge a fee when you use their platforms, but sometimes they offer discounts to traders who make a certain number of trades each month or those with funded accounts.

Examples of Swing Trading Platforms

The Home Trading System

The home trading system is an algorithm and trading software designed to improve performance. Using this system, you can expect to make smarter, faster, and better trading decisions. This particular platform comes with innovative features and a custom algorithm that combines seamlessly to provide a real-time, fully integrated trading platform. You are bound to benefit from this platform and experience the benefits of seamless trading complete with all the features that you need. The platform is completely compatible with some of the most dynamic and highly reliable charting tool. It is able to work with all kinds of markets, from stocks to Forex and indices. The platform is compatible with a variety of bars, such as range and momentum bars as well as tick charts.

The Entry Zone Platform

We also have a swing trading platform known as the Entry Zone. This platform has been around for a while but has recently undergone a complete overhaul. It has received a new design to address the needs of swing traders specifically. There is no trader in the entire world who wants to join an over-extended market even when it features a large stop-loss point. One of the main benefits of this specific platform is that it helps eliminate the challenge of entering an overly extended market. It starts by first checking for a pullback. It does this by accessing the 60-minute timeframe. This way, you will be protected from accessing the markets at the worst moment. The algorithm is able to proceed and track the markets so that you eventually get to find out the best market entry points.

Able Trend Trading Platform

This is another platform designed with swing traders in mind. One of its most outstanding features is its ability to identify changes in the trend instantly. Trend direction is first indicated by a distinct color. When the signal is headed upwards, then the color is blue; when it heads downwards, it changes color to red. If there is any sideways movement, then the color changes once more to green.

This platform, therefore, makes it pretty easy to observe the market trend and keep abreast of it. Additional information will then enable you to make the necessary trade moves that you need to as a swing trader. For instance, you will notice red and blue dots on your screen. These indicate the various stop points. When there is a downward trend, then the red dots will indicate your sell points while blue dots will indicate your buy points on the upward trend. These stop points ensure that you partake of the large market movements but with very little risk or exposure.

Interactive Brokers

This is a popular platform that has been recently revamped. It is a highly rated software because of the useful tools available to traders. Some of these tools are extremely useful for seasoned or sophisticated traders who need more than just the basics. This platform is able to connect you to any and all exchanges across the world. For instance, you may want to trade markets in Hong Kong, Australia, and so on. The software is able to connect you seamlessly so that you have a great trading experience.

This platform has seen the addition of new features which make trading even easier. These are, however, more suitable to seasoned traders who are more sophisticated than the average retail investor or small trader.

One of the attractive features of Interactive Brokers is that it is a very affordable platform to use. It is especially cost-friendly to small scale traders, retail investors, and the ordinary swing trader as the margin rates are low and affordable.

How to Buy and Sell Stocks

I f you are thinking of buying and selling stocks, you need a brokerage account. However, you cannot call a company to ask to buy their stocks. We know you are excited to make gains in the market. So, we are going to show you how you can start buying and selling stocks. There are three ways you can start trading stocks. They include:

1. Opening an account with full-service brokers

Have you ever seen a movie with sharply-dressed businesspeople sitting down with a client? Well, these are the traditional stockbrokers who talk to a client to get to know them both personally and financially. They are thorough at what they do to get to know you, they will ask about factors such as marital status, income, assets, liabilities, risk tolerance, time horizon and more, depending on what they need to know. They ask these questions because they want to know as much as they can to develop an investment strategy for you. They will give you different options depending on your investment needs to ensure your account remains profitable.

Furthermore, they also help you with other needs apart from your investment needs. Often you will find that these brokers provide services in areas such as tax planning, estate planning, budgeting, and retirement advice. These brokers are useful for individuals who seek to have all their investment needs to be catered for under one roof. Also, they help you manage your financial situation as you are now and in the long term. However, their services do not come cheap. For most full-service firms, you will have to part with 1,000 dollars or more to open an account with them. Besides, they offer great services in-house, which is a bonus for a first-time individual looking to sell or buy shares. They take their customer service seriously and will assign you as their client a financial advisor or broker who will be providing regular updates on your account and will act as the contact person between you and the firm.

The benefits of using this type of brokers to sell and buy socks include:

- They have large research departments with analysts who provide you with detailed reports and recommendations on moves to make.

- Also, if they have investment banking divisions, they will offer their clients access to IPOs (Initial Public Offerings), preferred stocks, debt instruments, and various alternative investment opportunities.

- You will also have security because they have physical offices where a client can visit to enquire about their portfolio performance.

- Also, some of these firms have online platforms where individuals can trade by themselves.

- They offer a one-stop-shop for all your investment and financial needs.

Cons

- Remember, brokers and financial advisors are sales representatives of the brokerage firm. So, no matter how well they treat you, they will be paid based on how much revenue they bring in. Watch out for their sweet talking and make a good decision based on their offerings.

- Sometimes their advice may be difficult to understand. Therefore, the next time you don't understand, ensure you seek explanations to the reasoning behind their suggestion.

- Do not be enticed to hand over your authority to the broker to buy and sell stocks for you. When something goes wrong, you will not have any recourse as you voluntarily handed over your authority for them to act on your behalf.

2. Online brokers

These are brokers interface with clients through the internet rather than in person. However, unlike full-service brokers, these companies do not advise your investments. They only take offers on which stock you want to purchase or sell. Additionally, they are cheaper than the full-service brokers because they have no offices you can visit or financial advisors you can interact with for advice. With this type of broker, you can set up an account over the internet for free or at a small cost. After opening the account on their website, you can access it and start selling and buying the stock immediately. However, when you deplete your account balance when you incur a loss, you will have to load more money on the online platform to continue trading.

Remember that these brokers will provide no advice on stocks or any type of investments whatsoever. They only assist in technical things, for example, when you have forgotten your password, or you have an issue setting up funds in the account. However, they will provide links to resources and research that can be useful in helping you make investment decisions. These types of accounts for selling and buying stock will be useful for people who are knowledgeable and are willing to take responsibility for managing their investments. Also, if you are a beginner and would like to teach yourself how to trade, these companies offer a demo account where you can sharpen your strategies before opening a funded account. If you feel you are knowledgeable to start trading on your own, this type of broker is for you.

The online brokers have distinct benefits as a platform for selling and buying stocks. They include:

- They have lower fees for opening accounts and transaction costs.

- You are in control of your account, and you can trade as you wish anywhere as long as you have an internet connection.

- You can also avoid brokerage bias. This is where a broker gives advice that benefits them in the form of commissions.

- You will have access to online resources and tools to optimize your trades.

- You monitor your investments in real-time.

Cons

- You could start investing too much too fast, which increases your risk of making a poor investment choice.

- If it is your first time to sell and buy stocks, autonomy can be overwhelming.

- It is dependent on the internet, so when you experience internet troubles, you could lose a potentially lucrative trade.

3. Direct Stock Purchase Plan (DSPP)

This is a type of special arrangement where the company (usually blue-chip firms), lets individual investors purchase stock directly from the company. DSPPs was conceived to allow an investor to avoid using a broker to purchase the stocks. Some of these companies make plans to sell these shares to individuals, but others prefer to contract third parties to administrate the transactions. You should know that not all blue-chip companies have these plans. However, when they offer these plans, they may have restrictions on when an individual may purchase the shares. Although with the increase in online platforms where you can trade, this plan offers long-term investors who do not have much money to spend on fees the convenience to start. Where can you find DSPPs? Companies that plan to issue shares using DSPP cite plans on the website under investor relations or under frequently asked questions page.

Pros of trading DSPPs

- You will get to buy a stock at lower fees by avoiding the costs that come up with setting up an account.

- Most companies offering stock using DSPPs sign up the stockholders for dividend reinvestment, and they can accumulate additional stocks at no extra cost.

- It allows for the fractional purchase of the stock. As

long as you have funds to initiate the position in a stock. The DSPP allows an investor to buy a fraction of the stock, which would otherwise be difficult through a broker.

Cons

- Stocks purchased through DSPPs are highly illiquid, meaning they are well suited for long term dividend investors. They are inconvenient in moving in and out of different stocks in a short time.

- When opening a DSPP account, you should know that it will be different from the one opened with your broker. Some investors find that having multiple accounts is inconvenient.

We know you can't wait to start trading, just remember investing is easy, but doing it successfully is tough. If you are not knowledgeable in investing using stocks, you have a high probability of losing your money. Before you start selling and buying a stock, you need to exhaustively do research on the stock you want to purchase. You need to know what kind of goods or services the company offers, how their flagship product is doing in the market, and the regions they operate from. Think of it as like going for a first date. You would probably want to know the things that matter before you decide to go out with the same person again.

So, what do you need to look at? Before you buy stocks, ask yourself for how long you are willing to hold on to them. If you are seeking to park your money in the market, it could earn you some dividends as time goes by. Be sure to check whether a company pays a dividend each year because you get paid regardless of the prevailing price of the stock. Also, you could look at what the company is offering in terms of revenue for every dollar you purchase in stock. You could start comparing their earning per year to their prevailing stock price if the price to earnings ratio is low, but they are in the growth stage; it is a share worth watching. Plus, you will buy it on the cheap, and if their growth picks up, you will realize some gains in the market.

Risk and Account Management

To be an active securities exchange broker, you should pursue a risk of the executive's plan. A chance, the executive's plan helps safeguard trading capital while procuring reliable returns. It likewise helps control your feelings while implementing self-restraint. The primary components of risk the board incorporate deciding the risk sum and position estimate, distinguishing the stop price, and looking at the risk/remunerate proportion.

Decide the Risk Amount

The risk sum is the most extreme sum you are happy to risk on some random exchange. It is typically a set level of your all-out record esteem. A typical principle guideline is to risk 1-3% of your complete record an incentive with each exchange. This sum ought to be diminished in times of high instability. In this way, a dealer with a capital of $50,000 that risks 2% per exchange would risk $1000 on each transaction.

Distinguish Stop Price

Before entering an exchange, you should set a stop misfortune price to help limit misfortunes and the impact of feelings. This price speaks to the dimension at which your position will be shut if the exchange moves against you. It will be activated consequently when the stock price exchanges at or past that dimension. Remember that slippage may happen, and you may lose more than you had at first determined. A stop misfortune request ensures execution; however, the price may move further against you before the exchange is executed.

Figure Position Size

When you have decided on the risk sum and stop price, you would then be able to ascertain several offers that you will exchange. This number, or position estimate, can be determined by partitioning the risk sum by the risk-per-share. The risk-per-share is the distinction between the stop price and the entry price. In this way, expect your most extreme risk sum is $1000 per exchange. If your entry price is $30 and your stop misfortune price is $28, at that point, the risk-per-offer would be $2. To ascertain the position estimate, straightforward separation $1000 by $2. Your position size would be 500 offers. Entry price $30 - Stop price $28 = $2 Risk-per-share

$1,000/$2 = 500 offers

Look at Risk/Reward

Looking at the risk/remunerate proportion is critical in deciding if a sensible benefit potential exists concerning the risk. It is an essential part of your general money, the executive's procedure. The reward-per-share is the contrast between the actual price and the entry price. The risk-per-share is the distinction between the entry price and the stop price. The risk/remunerate proportion ought to be set up before entering an exchange and ought to never be under 1:3. All together words, the benefit an incentive for each exchange arrangement must be in any event multiple times bigger than the risk esteem. When your entry price is $30, and your actual cost is $36, at that point the reward-per-offer would be $6. With a stop loss of $28, your risk/compensate proportion would be 2:6, or 1:3.

- Entry price $30 - Stop price $28 = $2 Risk-per-share

- Target price $36 - Entry price $30 = $6 Reward-per-share

- 2:6 = 1:3 Risk Reward Ratio

More Money Management Tips

For online day trading, just exchange stocks that have an average trading volume of more than 1,000,000 offers for the day. For swing trading, only exchange stocks that have an average trading volume of more than 300,000 suggestions for every day. Likewise, you should exchange stocks that are priced above $5. Specialized investigation may bomb on stocks underneath this price since they can be effectively controlled.

Synopsis

Understanding and following appropriate stock trading risk, the board rules will enable you to limit your misfortunes while acquiring steady returns. Carefully monitoring your money, the board standards will help keep the feeling out of the exchange.

Manual for Swing Trading Strategy

The swing trading system is regularly used to win benefits from transient price changes in the securities exchange. It is generally known as a successful system to expand benefits while acquiring insignificant risks and misfortunes. Picking the correct stock and the right market assumes an essential job in the swing trading system. Swing merchants generally choose stocks with outrageous vacillations. This trading procedure is usually executed if the market is steady. The steadiness of the market results in minor varieties in the cash price, which can be useful to swing brokers. The procedure isn't pertinent if the market is quickly rising or slamming.

Since it includes a shorter course of events and fewer risks, the swing day procedure is prevalent among dealers who are yet working their way in the outside cash advertise.

Trading in supplies of large organizations can result in higher benefits in a shorter span. Selling of these significant stocks, otherwise called enormous top stocks, as a rule, happens in stock trades. Taller varieties can be found in their prices contrasted with different stocks, along these lines inferring increment in benefits for the swing brokers. As a rule, a swing broker adheres to a specific stock as it increments in worth; however, he may move to another capital if the pattern changes. Along these lines, a swing trading methodology would possibly be fruitful if the correct stock has been picked. For a swing trading procedure to guarantee achievement and benefits for the swing broker, the decision of the market is likewise an essential factor. The development of the stock prices in a market with a rising or falling pattern takes a solitary course. This single course of evolution would prompt lesser gainful varieties for the swing broker. Steady demand is progressively fitting for swing brokers where its fall promptly trails the ascent of the record.

There are confinements to the arrangements you can take before the exchange. A level of risk shirking is additionally engaged with the procedure. In trading, you will, in the long run, become familiar with the art through a genuine encounter and presentation to risks and misfortunes. Swing merchants additionally utilize various methodologies and pursue alternate points of view. Consequently, the average return in swing trading enormously differs. Using a segment of the capital is a smart thought to oversee risks for the individuals who have just been in the field for a long while. However, it doesn't remain constant for the newcomers and amateurs. Taking positions that are more noteworthy than what your resistance for risk can deal with would be inconvenient to your presentation. Swing merchants should concentrate their endeavors and focus on producing the development of the price. In like manner, you ought to likewise be inspired to be a superior broker since that would involve more money coming in. New swing dealers are additionally not encouraged to put in a lot of money in their record for their underlying exchanges. It can bring a newcomer a higher number of misfortunes than additions. At the underlying stage, the most magnificent suggested capital is $35,000.00.

Risk Management—Stock Market

Numerous individuals ignore the significance of overseeing risk in their positions and exchanges. As a trader or financial specialist, this is the main thing that we can control. We can't control the bearings of the markets. We likewise can't control whether we will win or lose in any position we take. The main thing inside our control is the measure of misfortune we will endure.

To most traders, risk management implies essentially setting stops. Numerous financial specialists don't do this to control risk. In any case, there is considerably more to deal with your risk in the markets. You wouldn't drive onto an extension if you have seen that the more significant part of the backings has disintegrated, would you? OK, walk onto a solidified lake in the wake of seeing a "Slim Ice" signposted and a few breaks appearing in the ice itself? You wouldn't, that is because you watched the earth and understood that it was too risky to even think about proceeding.

We must watch a similar order when we are engaged with the money related markets. To dissect risk before exchanging or contributing, we should take a gander at the present market condition, the security's, and the pattern. Is it safe to say that we are in a risk recognize that would block us from taking an exchange? Assume the markets were bearish, your security has quite recently discharged frustrating profit and is close supply on your exchanging time frame. OK, purchase shares since costs climbed somewhat? Likely, you wouldn't. Even though you have a momentary bullish move, the staggering bearishness of the markets discloses to you that the earth is risky, and the reward isn't huge enough to embrace an extended position.

Numerous individuals can design an exchange; however, not all be able to break down the risk and deal with the threat in a way that guarantees their money-related survival in the markets when things turn out badly. Also, trust me, they will now and then.

There are two main risk management methods that I wish to examine here:

Recurrence

In exchanging and contributing, recurrence alludes to the number of positions we will open. The issue with numerous traders/speculators is that they will attempt to accept every single open entryway they see and public areas with just a minimal possibility for progress. They do this because of the dread of passing up on chances and profits in the markets.

Successful traders/speculators have the order to be increasingly particular in their opening of positions and take just those exchanges that meet explicit criteria laid out in their arrangement and that offer a high likelihood for profits. As another trader/financial specialist, you should constrain the number of exchanges you take. This will compel you to search for the correct chances to exchange as opposed to bouncing in on any little move in the markets. Keep in mind, regardless of whether you pass up on an opportunity, there is likely another tagging along very soon.

Duration

The following method is duration, or the measure of time spent in the position. The more you pay in an area, the higher the shot for unfavorable value development. This is the reason speculators go out on a limb in the markets than traders do. When we center around littler time frame diagrams, we have less profit potential yet besides, significantly less risk. Exchanging on littler time frames decreases the threat we face in our exchanges. This does not imply that we ought not to hope to profit from longer time frame positions. You can make up for the expanded duration risk by diminishing the other two elements of size or potentially recurrence. Longer-term traders and financial specialists can, in any case, oversee risk well.

The duration may likewise be turned down when instability in the markets rise. Rising uncertainty causes increasingly extraordinary cost swings. As another trader who is not used to exchanging these swings, you are best served by lessening your presentation to them by exchanging littler time frames.

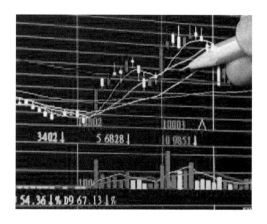

Technical Analysis – Charting Basics

One of the most important toolboxes for the swing trader is technical analysis. You don't have to become as much of an expert at it as a day trader would have to, but it's still very important to understand the basics and pick 2-3 tools to use in analysis to determine what trades to enter, what profit levels to shoot for, and what stop losses you should put in place to protect yourself. Technical analysis can put off a lot of people, but you aren't going to need to do any fancy math, everything is done for you, so all you need is a little bit of understanding of graphs and charts. Most of it is common sense, and you'll be looking for some transitions in your data. With swing trading, the number one error is not looking at the right time frames. You always need to keep your time frame in mind and remember that not all swing traders use the same time frames – so you need to focus on what is appropriate for your personal situation.

Moving Averages

Everyone understands the concept of an average. For the stock market, to get the average price, you simply add up the prices and then divide by the number of points. A moving average means that at each data point, you calculate the average from that data point backward for the number of time steps you want to use. So, if we were using a daily stock chart, a 7-day moving average would calculate the average for the past 7 days at each point and build up a curve using that data. The reason you want to do this is to smooth out the data into a nice curve, and that is going to give you a better idea of the trend in prices since it weeds out all the noise.

One downside about the moving average is that it's a lagging indicator. That means it's based on past pricing data. Obviously, we can't use a tool that gives us future pricing data. We don't know what that information is. Even so, moving averages give us surprising information that can be useful.

Moving averages used in the stock market analysis are either simple or exponential. What we described above is a simple moving average that is you just add up the number of data points you want and divide by the count.

So, if the price of a stock was $12, $14, $10, $12, and $13 over the past five days, the moving average on the fifth day would be:

MA = $(12+14+10+12+13)/5 = $12.20

If the following day the price is $14.25, the next moving average is:

MA = $(14+10+12+13+14.25)/5 = $12.65

On the stock chart, the value of the MA would be plotted at each point and the values connected into a smooth line. The purple line in this chart shows the 50 days moving average curve for AMD, plotted along with its actual share price.

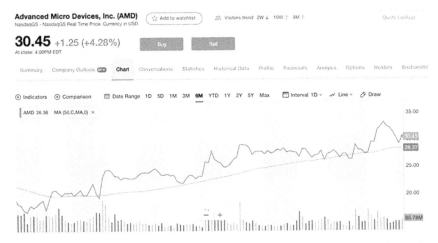

When you add a moving average to a chart, you can select the period and determine whether it uses closing price, open price, high, low, and several other options. Most of the time, we will use closing price and the period default (most commonly used value) is 50, which makes the moving average sensitive to prices over the past 50 periods while for a swing trader you'd be interested in days.

Benefits of Moving Averages

In technical analysis, moving averages are going to help you look at two important things. The first is they help identify trends. In a minute we'll see how you can do that. Second, they help you identify support and resistance levels. They do this far better than what you can do by simply drawing straight lines on your charts, even though we spent a lot of time doing that.

Exponential moving averages

You can also generate exponential moving averages. An exponential moving average has a complicated formula, so we aren't going to work through that part, you can simply use any stock website to add it to a chart. The important thing to remember about them is that they are more sensitive to recent prices. The reason is that the exponential moving average uses weighting that gives more recent prices more emphasis. That makes more sense, especially when you are a swing trader and more interested in shorter-term price changes. With a simple moving average, a price from two months ago has the same weight as yesterday's price, and that might not be relevant to you.

You can see this kind of movement in the chart below, which shows SPY over a one-year period. The purple line is a 50-day simple moving average, and the green line is the 200-day moving average. So, we are looking for points at which the purple line, or shorter-term moving average, crosses above or below the longer-term moving average (the green line).

You can clearly see that the purple line went below the green line before there was a major decline in the share price. So, had you been paying attention, you might have been able to take advantage of the situation either by shorting the stock or perhaps by investing in some put options.

Later, you will also notice that the short-term MA crossed back above the longer-term MA, perhaps indicating an uptrend. The dip you see in the chart is actually a short-term market decline that happened as a result of some tweets from President Trump, so it may not have any real significance related to the longer-term trends.

The data provided by a moving average isn't perfect, but you can use moving averages to estimate support and resistance levels. In an upward trend, a 50-day moving average will give you the support level for the data. So, it can be used to estimate what you should use for your stop-loss price. The position of the current price relative to the 50-day moving average will give you an indication of trend. In our examples, we are looking at past behavior, but you are going to want to look more at current behavior when trying to determine when to enter or exit trades. In the chart for Apple below, notice the position of the handles relative to the purple line, which gives the 50-day moving average.

When the trend is up, the candles are above the 50-day moving average. Then when the trend is down, notice that the candles are below the 50-day moving average. This can help you estimate what the current trend is. You should combine your estimate using this technique with data from other indicators.

Buy signals

When a short term moving average crosses above a longer-term moving average, that can be taken as a buy signal if you are hoping for a rising share price. Notice in this chart for Apple, the 10-day moving average has recently crossed above the 50 days moving average, possibly signaling a coming uptrend.

You can also observe from the chart that when the short term moving average crosses below the long-term moving average, you see a sell signal. Indeed, that played out with a declining share price.

Exponential versus Simple Moving Averages

As we said earlier, an exponential moving average is more sensitive to recent prices. Since an exponential moving average is more sensitive to recent prices, it might be able to give us faster insight into coming trend changes. That is, it will detect a trend change before a simple moving average. However, keep in mind that a lot of short-term fluctuations in share price are simply due to noise or random behavior. That means that an exponential moving average might give more weight to meaningless price fluctuations than it should.

In any case, a rising exponential moving average can be taken to indicate a rising share price and vice versa. A good buy signal with the exponential moving average is to look for a rising exponential moving average but with share prices below it. If the exponential moving average is declining, and the stock price dips below it, that might mean it's time to sell your shares.

Technical Analysis – Indicator

Tools

Technical analysis, a discipline utilized in trading, is used to assess investments and recognize opportunities for trading by evaluating statistical trends that have been collected from trading action. This includes elements such as volume and price movement. While fundamental analysis is meant to assess the intrinsic value of a security and the fairness of its price, we use technical analysis to identify signals, movement patterns, and other quantifiable data so that we can calculate the strengths and weaknesses of a security. We're not concerned with a company's financials. With technical analysis, we assume that a price already represents all known information.

Technical analysis can be utilized with a security as long as it has a history of trading data. Historical price changes and trading activity can effectively indicate probably price movements in a security's future. These securities can be stocks, commodities, futures, currencies, etc. The approaches of various technical analyses can be applied to all types of securities. Technical analysis is especially common with forex and commodities trading since they're both built upon price movements in the short term.

The goal of technical analysis is to predict the price movement of essentially anything that can be traded (and is affected by supply and demand). This includes stocks, currency pairs, bonds, and futures. In simplest terms, technical analysis is the study of securities' price movements and the impact supply and demand efforts thereof. Although price (specifically, price change) is the basis of technical analysis, some experts also observe and evaluate other quantities, such as interest figures and trading volume.

Researchers have cultivated hundreds of signals and patterns in their analysis. They've also created various trading systems that assist in price movement prediction. Some indicators identify a trend's strength and the probability it will continue. Others recognize trends, such as support and resistance, in the current market. Popular technical indicators include channels, moving averages, trendlines, and momentum indicators. Technical analysts observe six kinds of indicators:

- Chart patterns

- Oscillators

- Support and resistance levels

- Price trends

- Volume and momentum indicators

- Moving averages

Reading Charts

Stock charts can be line charts, bar charts, candlestick charts, or point and figure charts. Regardless of type, all stock charts have the following:

- Chart identification

- Summary key

- Time period

- Moving averages

- Volume

- Daily trade range

Reading a stock chart helps us analyze a stock's activity over time. You can find basic information on stocks in Google Finance. Remember that a stock's ticker symbol is represented by letters after the company's name. You can type the ticker symbol into the Google Finance search box. When the company's line chart comes up, you can click the "expand" button in the top right corner to see the chart in its entirety.

To read a stock chart, the first thing we'll do is find the trendline. It probably sounds like common sense — the trendline moves up or down — but let's look at it a bit more closely. We know that a stock's price can sometimes make a big move, either positively or negatively. It's important to always remember that you should not allow your emotions to guide your decision-making. Looking at the trendline is just the first step, and it's a way for you to gauge the general goings-on. Consider, for a moment, that you see a drastic price drop during a specific time period. It's wise to take a look at the events that occurred during that time period. For example, was there a shift in leadership within the company? Did the company attempt to expand in areas that we now know were unsuccessful? Typically, a strong company rebounds from setbacks like these. It's worth observing over time. Use the trendline to determine what needs a closer look.

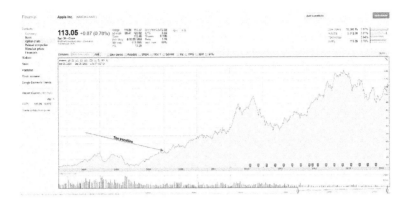

Support and Resistance

Support refers to a low level that a price reaches over a span of time; traders tend to buy when this happens. Resistance refers to a high level that it reaches over a span of time. When this occurs, traders tend to sell.

After you've examined the trendline, the next things to locate are lines of support and resistance. Over a given period of time, a stock will remain at certain levels. A level of support indicates a price below which a stock won't likely drop, while a level of resistance indicates a price above which a stock isn't likely to go. Lines of support and resistance are essentially barriers, and a stock's price fluctuates between them. The objective is to use these lines to know when to buy and when to sell.

Keep in mind that traders are likely to interpret a chart differently. Where you draw lines of support and resistance will depend on how long you intend to hold the stock (also known as your investment horizon). If you intend to hold a position for a long period of time, you might draw fewer lines of support and resistance than a trader who plans to hold a position for a very short time period. If you're planning to hold the position for a while, you're not concerned about every up and down. A short-term trader might draw more lines to evaluate trends in a shorter time span.

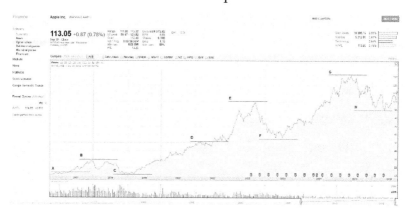

In this image, the first line of support is Line A. Line B is the first line of resistance. At Line C, you can see that the price has fallen, and we have a new level of support. After a substantial price increase, we have Line D, which is the next line of resistance.

Once we know the lines of support and resistance, it's easier to determine whether you should buy or sell a stock. Keep in mind that the lines are not objective; you'll draw them according to the anticipated length of your hold. Your judgment and evaluation are key.

Dividends and Stock Splits

If you look at the bottom of the chart, you'll notice if a company distributed a dividend. It will also tell you whether or not there was ever a stock split.

A dividend occurs when a board of directors for a company determines that they'll give a portion of profit to the shareholders. Anyone who owns stock will receive a small piece of the earnings. Not all companies issue dividends, but it shouldn't necessarily be the deciding factor when you're selecting a company in which to invest. Some companies prefer to reinvest earnings.

A stock split occurs when a board of directors decides to issue additional shares of stock to the public. I'd a company does a six-to-one split (written as 6:1), it means that for every share you own, you'll have six after the split. If you owned 300 shares, after the split, you'd own 1,800. The price might change, but the company's value doesn't. A stock split usually typically occurs when a share price doesn't align with competition. If the price of a share decreases, a company might do this to entice small investors. More investors increase demand, and in turn, the share price.

Trading Volumes

The little vertical lines at the bottom of the chart indicate a trend of volumes. While there are plenty of other factors to consider when purchasing stock, understanding volumes are always beneficial. Typically, a news story (either positive or negative) about a company will lead to a trading volume increase. As volumes increase, you might notice that a stock's price changes.

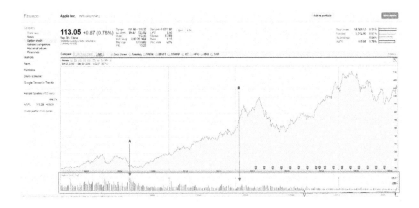

We can see that trading volume was high and there was also a dip in price at Line A. This chart doesn't indicate the reasoning behind this; however, we can guess that there was possibly an event that day that lead to panic. At Line B, there is a slight increase in volume coupled with an upward trend in price. (Volume and price don't always have a correlation; be careful not to assume there will always be one.) It's important to look at volume levels in the past compared to the present prior to making a decision. Increased volume generally means that buying and selling will be easy.

Technical Indicators

Technical indicators are an essential part of technical analysis. They are generally plotted on a chart to help us foresee a market trend. They essentially help us understand where the price is going. For example, a moving average (MA) is an indicator that is based on historical prices. It assists technical analysts with following trends, and it allows them to weed out small, short-term price movements.

MACD

Moving Average Convergence / Divergence (MACD) is an indicator that was created in the 1970s by Gerald Appel. It can also be called an oscillator, and it shows us various changes in factors such as strength, momentum, direction, and trend duration. It's essentially an assemblage of historical price data from three different times. The three series are the signal series (the average), the MACD series, and the divergence series (the difference between the other two series).

Exponential moving averages show us a stock's recent price changes. We use different lengths of time so that we can observe changes in the trend. Time periods a, b, and c are generally measured in days, and the values are typically 12, 26, and 9. You'll see it denotes as MACD (12,26,9).

We also look at crossovers. If a MACD crosses the signal line, it signifies that the acceleration is changing direction.

A zero crossover refers to the MACD series changing from positive to negative or vice versa. This occurs when there isn't a difference between the slow and fast EMAs. Changing from positive to negative is considered bearish while changing from negative to positive is considered bullish.

A positive (or bullish) divergence happens when a stock's price reaches a new low, but there isn't a new low on the MACD to verify it. A negative (or bearish) divergence happens when the price reaches a new high, but there isn't a new high on the MACD to verify it.

The MACD is efficient and helpful if it's used in the correct context. It's important to weed out false signals, which can result from any forecasting algorithm. For example, a quick decrease in a stock's price following a bullish crossover is known as a false positive. Conversely, a bearish crossover coupled with a sudden increase in a stock's price is known as a false negative. It's wise for technical analysts to utilize varying approaches to verify that the signals they're reading are true. It's wise to implement a filter to signal line crossovers because it will verify whether or not it remains.

Stochastics

Stochastics, which are relative strength indicators, help you recognize and identify market cycles and movement.

Market movement evolves through buy-and-sell cycles that can be identified through Stochastics (14, 7, 3) and other relative strength indicators. Buy-and-sell cycles typically peak when stocks reach levels that indicate they've been either overbought or oversold. They then reverse direction, and you'll see the two indicator lines cross over.

Price changes occur when forces (momentum, volume, etc.) combine. Generally, you won't see variations in security prices if the only adjustment is the market cycle. Instead, pay special attention to the bearish and bullish turns; they indicate who (buyers or sellers) are in control for that period.

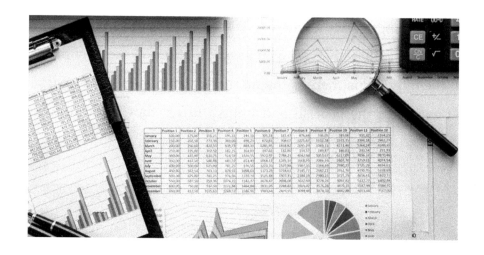

Swing Trading Guiding Principles

Swing trading is a type of trading in which you hold positions in stocks or other investments over a period of time that can range from 1 day to a few weeks or more. Before I discuss various strategies that can be used to swing trade, let's look at the basic guiding principles that I build these strategies on. They are as follows:

1. Keep it simple.

2. Treat your swing trading activity like a serious

business.

3. Develop a work plan and stick with it.

4. Actively manage your risk to reward ratio; focus on the entry.

5. Measure your results and adjust accordingly.

Keep it Simple

You may have heard of the term "paralysis by analysis." This happens when you analyze something to the point where you cannot make a decision. Some swing traders overcomplicate their analysis of a security by using multiple indicators that all have to line up for them to enter a trade. In real life, everything does not often line up perfectly and you have to go with what you feel is right.

I have thus far covered many different tools and indicators you can use to help you to make a decision. You do not need to use all of them to be a successful swing trader. Once you find 1 or 2 that work well for you, you should then stick with those. If you decide to use a few different tools that all need to align, it will likely mean that you are not going to be trading very often. That is not necessarily a bad thing, though. It is better to sit on your hands and wait for a good trade versus jumping in and out of marginal trade setups and slowly lose your money. The only one who wins, in that case, is your broker, as they collect fees for all your trades (the successful ones and the losing one's).

Find several indicators that work well for you and focus on using them. Don't trade often, but trade smart, by knowing why you are entering a trade and, most importantly, knowing your risk to reward ratio and exit price points. As you gain more experience in swing trading, you will be able to better recognize trades that are going to work out even if everything is not perfectly aligned.

Having said this, when you do happen to find a number of indicators that are all aligned with the trade you are considering taking, it can certainly provide some level of confidence that you have a potentially profitable trade.

Treat your Swing Trading Activity Like a

Serious Business

Should you decide that swing trading is a right fit for your personality, and that it is able to fit into your life along with all of your other interests and responsibilities, then you need to treat this activity as a very serious business. It will require an investment of time and effort, which hopefully will lead to some very good rewards.

Have a designated area where you do your research and keep all of your records. You are essentially becoming a professional money manager for yourself, so you should keep your work organized at all times. Everything you do with your business should be oriented toward making sure you are a success. If you feel like a professional, then you are more apt to trade like one.

Develop a Work Plan

Have a work plan and stick with it. Your work plan should include checking the market at the open and before the close. During this time, you should monitor your positions, set alerts, and possibly enter orders at target levels that you think might get filled during the trading day.

I also recommend that you evaluate your portfolio and market performance every night from Sunday to Thursday to ensure your assumptions about your positions and portfolio are still valid. On the weekend, you should try to do a more thorough assessment.

It is important to establish a work plan and keep it consistent. By keeping your work plan relatively consistent, you can measure your performance without introducing additional variables. Measuring your performance allows you to find areas to improve and make changes as you see fit.

Actively Manage your Risk to Reward Ratio, Focus on the Entry

As a swing trader, your first and most important tool is your capital or cash. As I have said before, without cash, you cannot be a trader. I have written at length already about the necessity of assessing the risk to reward ratio on every trade and also on how much capital you should put into each trade. Following your rules on these points will prevent you from quickly losing all of your capital. You will be wrong on your trades some of the time and you need to make sure you live to trade another day.

Just planning and knowing your stop-loss and profitable exits are not enough for swing trading. Your entry becomes the following important step in your trade. You have already determined your stop-loss point and your target price(s) for a profitable exit. However, you calculated the risk to reward ratio based on an assumed entry price point.

Let's assume you found a good setup during a scan in the evening after the market has closed. The security closed the day at $10.50 and you see an upside to $12.00 with support at $10.00 where you would stop out. Therefore, you have a potential $0.50 loss compared to a $1.50 gain to the upside. That is a 1 to 3 risk to reward ratio, which is very good, and you are ready to pull the trigger and place a buy order in the morning. The market opens the following morning and the security you are ready to buy opens up at $11.00. What do you do? The novice trader is already invested mentally in the trade, so they buy. Unfortunately for them, their risk to reward is now 1 to 1 with the downside to $10.00 and upside to $12.00. This is no longer a good trade at that entry point.

The rational trader reassesses the situation. They may put a buy order in at $10.50, hoping to catch the entry they wanted on the security during the normal daily price gyrations in the market. This will give them the risk to reward ratio that they need to make a good swing trade. If they do not get a fill, then they need to reassess again, and maybe move on to finding another trade with a more appropriate risk to reward ratio.

The bottom line does not get emotional and chase a trade. The "fear of missing out" can motivate you to make a bad trade and you should be aware of this when picking your entry price on a trade.

Measure your Results and Adjust Accordingly

As a trader, you must track your results to measure your performance. Nothing gets improved that does not get measured first. Every trader should use a tool to record the different aspects of each trade, from initial assessment through to the risk to reward expected, the entry point, and, finally, the exit. The tool can be a spreadsheet, it can be done on paper or it can be web-based. It does not matter how you do it as long as the process allows you to track the details of each trade as well as your performance.

Once you have your trades recorded in detail, you can go back at any time and evaluate how the trade worked. You can compare your performance on using the different indicators, i.e., is one working particularly well versus the others that you use? Are you getting good entry points on your trades or do you need to exercise more patience? Are your exits working or are you consistently exiting a trade too early and not getting all of the money you could on a profitable trade? Are you respecting your stops?

Having all of this information to evaluate will help you adjust your trading process and plan accordingly to maximize your performance without letting emotion enter into your decision-making.

Summary

- Keep your strategies relatively simple. There are lots of tools available and much analysis that you can do, but the more you include, the less likely you will find alignment on all of them. Focus on finding and using several tools that work for you.

- Focus on finding and trading only what you consider to be high-quality setups. You do not have to trade often to make a good return on your money.

- Develop a consistent work plan and routine that you follow. Try to keep your trading process and procedures consistent so that you can measure your results without introducing other variables.

- Make sure your trades are offering a good reward to the risk that you are taking. Manage the size of the risk that you are taking, so a large part of your capital is not at risk. Honor the levels you have decided to exit a trade if it does not work out the way you had hoped.

- Measure and assess your results regularly using a

journaling process.

- Adjust your trading plan or strategies if something stops working. The market constantly changes as sectors come in and out of favor and overall trends change. Be prepared to change and adjust to the market.

Swing Trading Strategies

ike with any other version of trading, there are various strategies that you can use throughout your trading career. While most people like to stick to one or two strategies, which means they have to find financial instruments that work with their chosen strategies, other traders tend to go from one strategy to the next. However, as a beginner, it is best to realize that you should stick with one strategy as this will help you continue to learn about swing trading and how the stock market works in general. Of course, as you continue to build your trading knowledge and become more comfortable with swing trading, you can look into other strategies.

Trend Following

No matter what strategy you decide to use, you will need to make sure that you understand how to read charts and trend lines. You will use these tools in order to help guide you towards the best time to make your move to buy and sell a stock. When it comes to following a trend, there are a lot of details, such as what the opening price was, the highest price, the lowest price, and the closing price. You will analyze the trend over a period of time, how long depends on your personal preference. Through your analysis, you will start to notice a pattern in the trend line. This is the pattern that you will follow when you decide to take on a stock, see if your strategy will work for the stock, or what strategy to use.

The factors that you will look at when trend following are:

Price of the Stock

The price of the stock is one of the most important features that you will pay attention to. This doesn't just mean the price of the stock at that moment, such as what you would pay in order to purchase the stock. Even though the current price is the most important price, you will want to pay attention to all of the prices that you see for every day that you take into your analysis. For example, if you decide to look at the historical context of the last two months, you will look at about 60 days of stock pricing in order to help you find a trend. This means that you will look at the opening price for each of these days, the closing price, the highest price, and the lowest price. You will want to look at these prices in detail and in general. In a sense, this means that you will look at the larger image and the smaller pieces that make up, the larger image.

Managing Your Money

Money management is thought to be one of the trickiest parts of trading. When it comes to managing your money, you want to make sure that you don't have too much money as it can give you a bigger loss. However, if you have too little money for the stock, then you aren't able to reach the full benefits when you make the trade. This is another time in swing trading when you want to find the best spot in order to make the trade.

One of the biggest tips to help you figure out how much money to put towards a stock is by evaluating the risks associated with the stock. You will be able to do this through any strategy that you will use and various other factors that are part of your trading plan.

Rules and Guidelines

One of the most important factors to remember when you are looking towards your trend line and thinking of making a trade. These rules are not only the guidelines that you will receive as you start to learn the swing trading technique, but they are also the rules that you will set for yourself. For example, if you decide that your stop-loss price is going to be $10.00 lower than the price you bought the stock from, you will want to make sure that you follow this guideline.

One of the biggest reasons you need to make sure that you are following your guidelines is because the more consistent you are with your trading, the more likely you are to become successful. Furthermore, you will want to make sure that you follow the guidelines as they will help you to think systematically when it comes to making decisions. While you might find yourself turning back to your trading plan and guidelines consistently as a beginner, the more you follow the same procedures, the more you will focus on them as a way in making sure you are following the steps instead of needing them more for direct reference on where to go and what to do next. In a sense, trading will start to become more natural to you, which is a great strength when you are analyzing trend lines.

Diversity

Diversity is one of the more popular controversies when it comes to trading. While some traders feel you need to have great diversity, which is a variety of stocks, in your portfolio, others feel that this isn't as important. In reality, the more serious you want to be with your trading, the more you will focus on diversity. However, this isn't always true when it comes to investors. But, as stated before, investing and trading are two different career paths in the stock market.

You can look at diversity as what is the right feature for you. You might find that you don't need to have a large diversity because you are a part-time swing trader, or you have a specific target that you focus on. However, you might also find that the more diversity you have, the better-rounded you feel as a trader. You might find that diversity is helping you learn more about investing in general.

Always Note the Risk

Another important factor to pay attention to when you are looking into trend following is how much risk is involved if you decide to take on the financial instrument you are looking at. When you are looking at the risk, you always have to pay attention to your guidelines and your trading plan. These two factors will help you decide if you should take on the stock due to the risk it carries or not. It is important to remember you need to stick to the risk level you are comfortable with. Even if you think that this stock could give you good rewards, this doesn't mean that you should agree to take on the financial instrument if you are uncomfortable with the risk.

This also doesn't mean that you can't increase your risk level as time goes on. You just want to make sure that you build your confidence and comfort level with risk as your risk grows. Furthermore, as you get more knowledgeable about swing trading, it might be a good thing to slowly increase your risk when it comes to taking on stocks. It's always good to grow in many directions as a trader, including with risk.

Trend following tends to be one of the most popular techniques when it comes to trading because it has a high success rate, providing you understand where the trend line is heading. Of course, you should always remember that the stock market can take drastic turns, and no one can truly predict the future. This means, even if you analyze the trend lines to the best degree, you will still have some risk involved as the trend line could differ a bit from what you originally thought.

Using Options as A Strategy

Because you are able to set up an agreement which gives you the option to buy or sell the stock later, you are technically strategizing the right time to take the next step in the future.

One of the biggest ways to do this is by analyzing the various charts that you see for your stock. In fact, you will focus a lot on technical analysis. You will focus on the historical charts of the stock as this will give you a timeframe for when you will want to take the next step.

Options are known to be a great strategy if you are looking for leverage, which is when you increase a return on a trade through borrowed money. It is important that you need to make sure you will only use this strategy if it helps you to receive more of a profit. In fact, this is one of the most important factors in choosing a strategy. You have to make sure that it is going to help you gain a profit and decrease your risks.

Short Interest

Many experienced traders state that beginners should not take part in the short interest strategy as it tends to be more of a guessing game than other strategies. When you focus on the short interest strategy, you will compare the number of short shares to the number of floating shares.

This is a great strategy to learn as a swing trader because it can show when the stock market is about to go into bearish conditions, which means that the stock prices will start to go down. Furthermore, short interest can also warn you about short   squeezing.

Pay Attention to The Float

One of the best ways that you can tell if a trade is going to help you is through a technique known as float. Basically, a float is the total number of shares that a trader will find in public sharing. This can become very helpful because, if you have the right size of float, you can see higher profits.

However, this is also the trick when it comes to the float strategy. There tends to be a fine line between having a massive float and having a float that will give you the best profits. The reason why a massive float, which would be too many shares, can cause you to lose capital instead of increasing your profits is because if you have a huge float, the price won't move as quickly. However, if you have a smaller number of shares in your float, then you will find that the price moves a bit higher, of course, this gives you a larger profit. With this said, you also don't want to have too little shares in your float. If this happens, then you won't be able to make much of a profit either as this can stop your float from increasing in price.

Breakout and Breakdown Strategies

When you focus on the breakout strategy, you are looking at the history of your stock's trend line in a microscopic fashion. What I mean by this is you will be focusing on what the trend has done over the past few days. When you are looking at the trend line, you will see every time the price has gone up and down. Stock prices are almost constantly changing throughout the day, which is what the trend line shows. Every now and then, you will notice in the trend line that you have several high points and several low points. These high points indicated the highest prices of the stock and the lowest points show the lowest prices.

The biggest difference between the breakout strategy compared to the breakdown strategy is the condition of the market. If you notice that the stock has been going on an upward trend for a while, you will use the breakout strategy. However, if you notice that the trend shows the price has been decreasing over time, you will use the breakdown strategy.

Of course, for both strategies, there is that specific spot you need to try in order to gain your best profit. The best spot to make your next move will depend on the pattern of the trend.

The Routine of a Swing Trader

Swing trading goals are, in many ways, different from other forms of trading. Day trading, for instance, is often a trader's sole occupation and so the goals include living needs. Swing traders often have another occupation elsewhere and only trade occasionally.

For most swing traders, cash is often not a problem because they have additional sources of income, such as employment, investments, or business. To make really big money, traders need to be well prepared.

Why Swing Trading?

Swing trading constitutes a trading strategy where traders enter positions and exit only after a certain period of time. This period of time ranges from at least two trading sessions to a couple of months. While swing trading gains may be smaller, they can add up to significant amounts over time.

Swing traders target profit margins of between 5% and 10% rather than the 20% to 25% margins. While such margins may not be impressive to some, they do add up over time. Traders searching for 20% - 25% and higher gains often invest more time into their trades, sometimes running into many months. They are often considered to be investors rather than traders because of the time factor. Basically, it is a lot more attractive to make 10% gains each week than 25% each month.

Swing traders take on average between 5 and 10 days. As such, it is possible to make lots of small money amounts, which then add up the course of a trading month. Swing traders, therefore, tend to make more money in the 5 to 10 days trading sessions compared to investors and to other traders as well.

Factor in Both Profits and Losses

Most traders set out believing they will win all trades. Sadly, this is not how things are in the real world. Traders actually lose out on some trades. Not even the most brilliant and most successful traders win all their trades. The important factor to keep in mind is to keep the losses to a minimum while maximizing on profitability.

Prudent money management techniques, as well as a proper state of mind, are essential ingredients in keeping losses at a minimum. Small gains are great over a certain period, but this can only be maintained if the losses are adequately managed. For instance, if you are to have stop-loss points, then position these at 2% to 3% rather than the usual 7% to 8%. This way, you will limit your losses and enhance your winnings. You will also manage the desirable trading ratios of 3 to 1 profit – loss ratios. These are crucial points to note because it takes just one large loss and an account could be wiped away. Major losses eat away at a trader's capital, which will affect subsequent trades. Swing trading can present excellent individual gains to a trader. Also, partial profits can be taken from a trade which is then allowed to continue its run.

Swing traders use both fundamental analysis and technical analysis to determine stocks with an upward trend and with momentum. A swing trader's work includes the identification of financial instruments such as stocks that have a well-defined trend.

The aim of a swing trader is to purchase securities when the prices are low, hold the securities for a couple of days, and then exit when the prices are high. This way, they exit trades profitably and it is the method that they use to earn their profits. It makes sense to enter trades when prices are low and then sell when the prices go up.

Trading Techniques

Swing trading techniques are easy to learn. They are also straightforward and simple to demonstrate. After learning these techniques, it is advisable to put them to practice for a couple of days until you get confident enough to trade live. If your practice trades were largely successful, then trading the real markets will also likely prove to be successful.

As a swing trader, you do not have to focus your energies using complicated formulas and learning complex techniques. You also do not need to buy and hold stocks or other financial instruments like currencies. Instead, you only need your trading charts.

Swing Trading compared to Day Trading

Swing trading is very similar to day trading. The major difference is time. Swing traders last much longer in positions taken while day traders last, on average, only a couple of minutes. They exit their trades fairly quickly and never hold positions overnight. As such, they avoid exposure to overnight risks.

There are certain risks in holding positions overnight as swing traders do. For instance, major events could take place that could hurt a position. Also, positions can change overnight based on any of a number of factors. However, day traders are also exposed to certain risks. For instance, huge spreads between ask and bid, as well as commissions, can seriously eat into profits. This is a problem for swing traders as well, but day traders have it much worse.

Also, there is a huge difference between day and swing traders when it comes to time commitment. Day traders are practically glued to their screens and cannot afford to multitask. A few moments' distractions and a trade could be lost. The amount of focus and dedication needed is extremely high. This is extremely different from what swing traders go through. Swing traders can enter a position and then head out to attend to other activities. The difference here is that swing traders have a lot of latitudes and can head off to attend to other duties. Day traders are practically occupied with trading and cannot attend to other matters at the same time.

Retail versus Professional Traders

As a retail trader, you may be at a disadvantage compared to professional traders. Professional traders are generally more experienced, have a lot of leverage, access to more information, and pay lower commissions. However, you do have some advantages in some instances because you are not limited to the risks that you can take, size of investment, and types of trades. As a retail swing trader, you need to ensure that you have all the knowledge necessary to take full advantage of the markets. Day traders lack a regular paycheck, especially retail, self-employed traders. They have to practically work hard and sweat in order to earn a living. Swing traders can withstand not trading or being away from the markets. It is generally not a matter of life and death to them. This is another major difference between the two.

How to Identify Potential Trades

So, how do you find trades that you'd be interested in? As a swing trader, you may want to find a catalyst. A fundamental catalyst will enable you to enter a trade with sufficient momentum. Then all you will need is technical analysis to confirm your exit and profit points.

1. Special opportunities: There are different ways of entering the market. One of these is to find a great opportunity with lots of potentials. Great opportunities can be found through companies planning an IPO, those ready to file for bankruptcy, situations of takeovers, buyouts, insider buying, mergers, acquisitions, and restructuring. These and other similar events provide excellent trading opportunities, especially for swing traders.

To find these opportunities, you need to check out the SEC website or filings from companies. Certain forms, such as 13-D and S-4 contain all the relevant information that you need. You can also subscribe to the website www.SECFilings.com so as to receive notifications whenever companies file reports. While these opportunities carry some inherent risks, the possible rewards are too great to ignore.

2. Sector or industry opportunities: Apart from the rare opportunities, we also have opportunities that are specific to a given sector. These are opportunities that you will find on certain websites regarding sectors whose performance is well above average. For instance, we can determine that sectors such as energy are doing exceptionally well by observing energy ETFs. There are certain sectors that pose a high risk but have high returns and can be very profitable.

3. Chart breaks: We can also rely on chart breaks to find opportunities. Chart breaks are especially suitable for swing traders. Chart breaks are really stocking or securities that have been traded so heavily such that they are awfully close to major resistance or support levels. As a swing trader, you will search for opportunities out there by identifying patterns indicating breakdowns or breakouts.

These identifying patterns can be Gann or Fibonacci levels, Wolfe Waves, channels, and triangles. However, please note that these chart breaks are only useful when there is huge interest in the stock. This way, you can easily enter and exit trades. Therefore, whenever you note this chart breaks, you should also focus on factors such as price and volumes.

Have a Securities Watch List

One of the things that you really should embark on is building a list of stocks or other securities to watch closely. The stocks that should constitute this list include those with a great chance at high volumes and upward price movement. It should also include stocks with a major catalyst.

Confirm your Current Positions

It is important to keep tabs on your current positions. You probably have other trades, so take a look at these and see if there is anything needed on your part. This is something that you should focus on early before the trading day begins. You should review these positions with the benefit of foresight based on the information obtained from news sources and online sites. See if any news items will affect your current positions.

Checking this out is pretty easy and straight forward. All that you need to do is to enter the stock symbol into websites such as www.news.google.com. This will reveal plenty of essential information that you need to be successful. Should you come across any material information that can directly affect your trades, then consider what you should do, such as adjusting the different points like take profit and stop-loss.

Trading During Market Hours

Now that the markets are open, it is time to get busy as a trader. During this time, you will mostly be trading and watching your screen. Check the market makers of the day and also be aware of any fake bids and asks.

Find a viable trade and apply all the skills and knowledge you have acquired to identify entry and exit points. There are plenty of techniques you can apply to arrive at these points. Think about Fibonacci extensions, for example. These can help you identify entry and exit points; you can also use price by volume and resistance levels.

As the trading day proceeds, you may need to make certain adjustments to your positions. These adjustments will depend on a number of factors. However, it is not advisable to adjust positions once you enter a trade, especially if you are planning on taking on additional risks. If you must adjust, then it is better to focus more on adjusting the take profit points and stop-loss levels.

After Hours Trading

Most swing traders are largely inactive after the normal trading day is over. At this point in time, the market is not liquid at all, and the available spread not suitable to enter any trades. Therefore, take this time to do some evaluation of your earlier trades and your positions. Examine your trades and see where you could do better. Focus on any open positions you may have and consider all material events that could have some effect on your positions.

Ingram Content Group UK Ltd.
Milton Keynes UK
UKHW050857040623
422772UK00008B/25

9 781803 623542